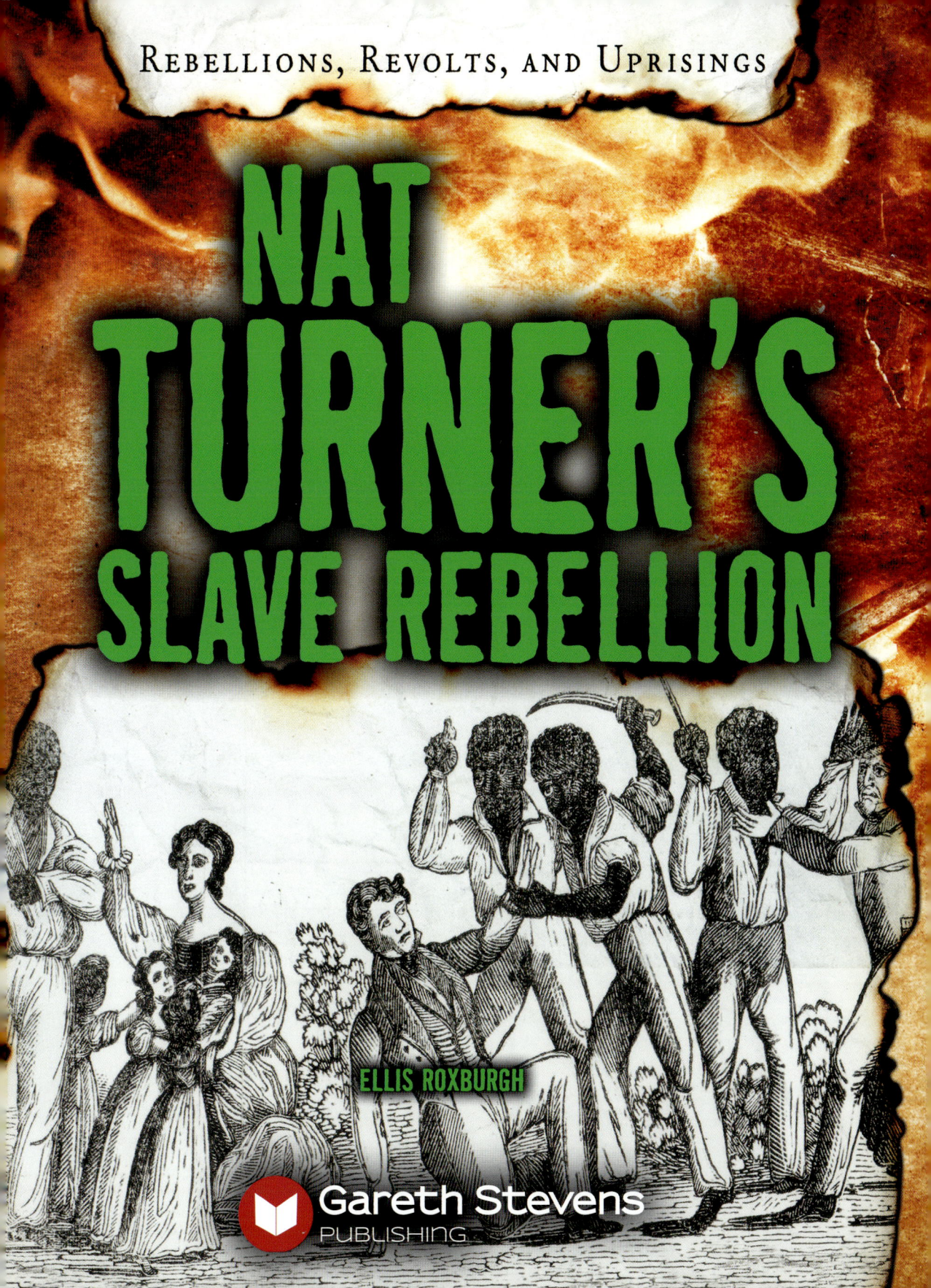

Please visit our website, www.garethstevens.com. For a free color catalog of all our high-quality books, call toll-free 1-800-542-2595 or fax 1-877-542-2596.

CATALOGING-IN-PUBLICATION DATA
Names: Roxburgh, Ellis.
Title: Nat Turner's slave rebellion / Ellis Roxburgh.
Description: New York : Gareth Stevens Publishing, 2018. | Series: Rebellions, revolts, and uprisings | Includes index.
Identifiers: ISBN 9781538207758 (pbk.) | ISBN 9781538207659 (library bound) | ISBN 9781538207536 (6 pack)
Subjects: LCSH: Turner, Nat, 1800?-1831--Juvenile literature. | Southampton Insurrection, 1831--Juvenile literature. | Slaves--Virginia--Southampton County--Biography--Juvenile literature. | Slave insurrections--Virginia--Southampton County--History--19th century--Juvenile literature. | Southampton County (Va.)--History--19th century--Juvenile literature.
Classification: LCC F232.S7 R69 2018 | DDC 975.5'5503092--dc23

Published in 2018 by
Gareth Stevens Publishing
111 East 14th Street, Suite 349
New York, NY 10003

Copyright © 2018 Gareth Stevens Publishing

For Brown Bear Books Ltd:
Managing Editor: Tim Cooke
Design Manager: Keith Davis
Editorial Director: Lindsey Lowe
Children's Publisher: Anne O'Daly
Picture Manager: Sophie Mortimer

Picture Credits
Cover: Getty: Fotosearch
Interior: Horst Auctioneers: 23; Library of Congress: 4, 11, 26, 30, 32, 34, 41, 43; Library of Virginia Special Collections: 33, 35; NASA: 19, 21; National Geographic: 42; Public Domain: 13, 25, Joel Bradshaw 27, 39 New York Public Library 16, River Brink Art Museum 31, Lyn Topinka/CVO Photo Archive 22, York Public Library/Granger 15, Virginia Encyclopedia 28, Virginia Foundation for the Humanities 40; Shutterstock: Everett Historical 5, 7, 9, 10, 14, 38, Joseph Sohm 8; Smithsonian National Museum of African American History and Culture: 18, Gift of Maurice Person and Noah and Briooke Porter 17; SuperStock: The Granger Collection 29; Thinkstock: istockphoto 20, thom Morris 8; University of Virginia Special Collections: Widener University 24, 36, 37.

All other images Brown Bear Books

Brown Bear Books has made every attempt to contact the copyright holder. If anyone has any information please contact licensing@brownbearbooks.co.uk

All rights reserved. No part of this book may be reproduced in any form without permission in writing from the publisher, except by a reviewer.

Manufactured in the United States of America

CPSIA compliance information: Batch #CS17GS. For further information contact Gareth Stevens, New York, New York at 1-800-542-2595.

CONTENTS

Roots of Rebellion 4
Who Were the Rebels? 12
Rebellion! 20
Fighting Authority 28
Defeat and Legacy 36

Timeline 44
Glossary 46
Further Information 47
Index 48

WORDS IN THE GLOSSARY APPEAR IN **BOLD** TYPE THE FIRST TIME THEY ARE USED IN THE TEXT.

ROOTS OF REBELLION

By the time the slave Nat Turner led a revolt in Virginia in 1831, the Southern states had come to rely on slave labor to work on the plantations. Despite this, there was growing opposition to slavery in the United States.

The first African slaves in America had arrived in 1619 at Jamestown, Virginia. Since then, the number of slaves had grown hugely. By 1830, however, **slavery** was largely limited to the South. Southerners called it their "peculiar institution." They argued that people in the North did not understand it. In the South, slaves worked

A family of slaves outside their hut in Virginia in 1862.

on cotton and tobacco **plantations**, in homes, on small farms, or in factories. There were about two million slaves in the South. They belonged to their owners, who treated them as pieces of property.

A Peculiar Institution

Slaves were usually taken from their villages in Africa by African or Arab traders. They were forced to march to trading posts on Africa's west coast. There, they were sold to traders from European countries such as Great Britain, and transported across the Atlantic Ocean in slave ships. In the Americas, they were sold to new owners.

A slave trader checks the health of a slave in Africa.

A Life in Captivity

On plantations in the South, slaves generally lived in families or other groups in small huts. After work, the slaves spent their time there cooking and resting. They relaxed by singing or playing music. Owners often made their slaves go to church on Sundays. Many slaves practiced a religion known as Santeria, which combined Christian teachings with elements of traditional African religions. Owners encouraged slaves to form families, because their children would become slaves in turn. These young slaves provided extra labor or were sold. Families were frequently split up when one or more members were sold.

These slave huts stand on a plantation in South Carolina.

Life in America

By the late 17th and early 18th centuries, slaves had no rights. The laws that protected slavery denied slaves the right to earn money or own property. The laws were based partly on a belief that black Africans were inferior to white Americans and partly on the fact that slavery was necessary to the South. The agricultural **economy** there had come to depend on large numbers of Africans working without pay. Most slaves worked on large plantations. Crops such as tobacco and cotton required many workers for planting, harvesting, and processing the harvest.

Slaves who fell sick on the voyage from Africa were thrown overboard to drown.

Slave owners lived in luxurious homes on their plantations.

Life on the Plantation

The quality of a slave's life on a plantation depended to a large extent on the owner. Some owners were kind and treated their slaves well. They included, for example, Nat Turner's first owner, Benjamin Turner. Such owners often allowed their slaves to learn to read and write and they did not whip them. But most slave owners treated their slaves harshly and used violence to force them to work. They would not let them learn to read and write. They were frightened that slaves might use written messages to encourage each other to rebel against their owners.

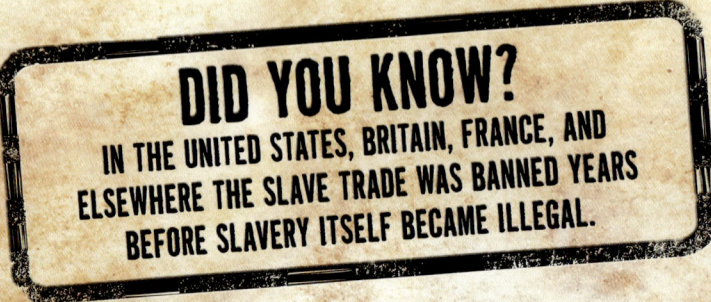

DID YOU KNOW?
IN THE UNITED STATES, BRITAIN, FRANCE, AND ELSEWHERE THE SLAVE TRADE WAS BANNED YEARS BEFORE SLAVERY ITSELF BECAME ILLEGAL.

A Slave Economy

In the South the economy was based on growing cotton, tobacco, and sugar. Such crops grew well in the subtropical climate. They required a lot of labor, however, so slaves were used to provide free labor. Although most of the slaves on a plantation worked in the fields, a small number were employed to work in the owner's home. Usually, working in the house was easier than working in the fields.

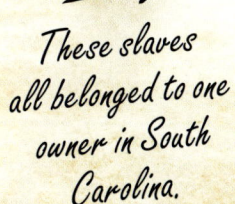

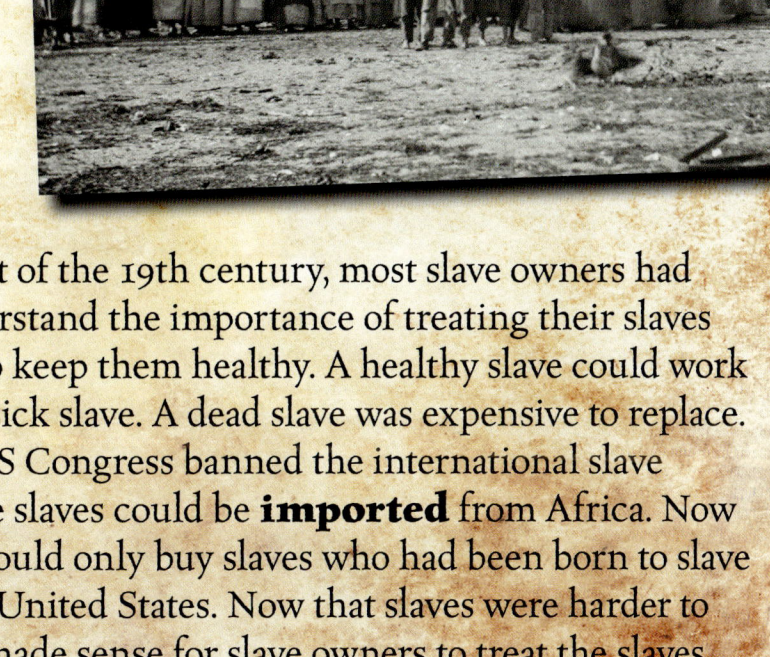

These slaves all belonged to one owner in South Carolina.

By the start of the 19th century, most slave owners had begun to understand the importance of treating their slaves well enough to keep them healthy. A healthy slave could work harder than a sick slave. A dead slave was expensive to replace. In 1808, the US Congress banned the international slave trade. No more slaves could be **imported** from Africa. Now slave owners could only buy slaves who had been born to slave parents in the United States. Now that slaves were harder to get hold of, it made sense for slave owners to treat the slaves they owned better than they had done before.

Opposition to Slavery

The new state of Ohio had abolished slavery in its constitution in 1802. **Abolitionists**, who opposed slavery, demanded to see it outlawed across the United States. By 1830, industry was growing in the North. As factories opened, machines did work previously done by people, so the need for slaves fell. Also, many Northerners were turning against slavery under the influence of religious groups such as the Quakers.

The cotton gin was invented in 1794. It procssed cotton far quicker than previously.

PICKING COTTON ON A GEORGIA PLANTATION.

Slaves harvest cotton on a Southern plantation.

The South

New inventions such as the **cotton gin** and the sewing machine had increased the demand for Southern cotton both at home and abroad. That led to a need for more slaves to pick the cotton in the fields.

As slavery came under growing attack from Northerners, some Southerners changed their argument in support of slavery. They had previously said it was a **necessary evil**. By the 1830s, many argued that slavery was a positive good. They said that slaves benefited from being owned by white Southerners. Some Southerners even claimed that God wanted them to keep slaves because, in their eyes, they had a Christian duty to free Africans from their traditional beliefs. This view was clearly **racist**, but it dominated the views in the South, where Nat Turner grew up.

WHO WERE THE REBELS?

From an early age, Nat Turner believed he had been chosen to carry out an important task. However, it took him some time to work out what that task was.

Nat Turner (1800–1831) was born into slavery in Southampton County, Virginia, on October 2, 1800. His mother had been bought in 1799 by a plantation owner named Benjamin Turner, from whom Nat took his surname. Nat's father was another slave. As a child, it was soon clear that Nat was smart. By the age of just 3 or 4 years old, he could describe in detail events that had happened before he had been born.

This illustration imagines how Nat Turner may have looked.

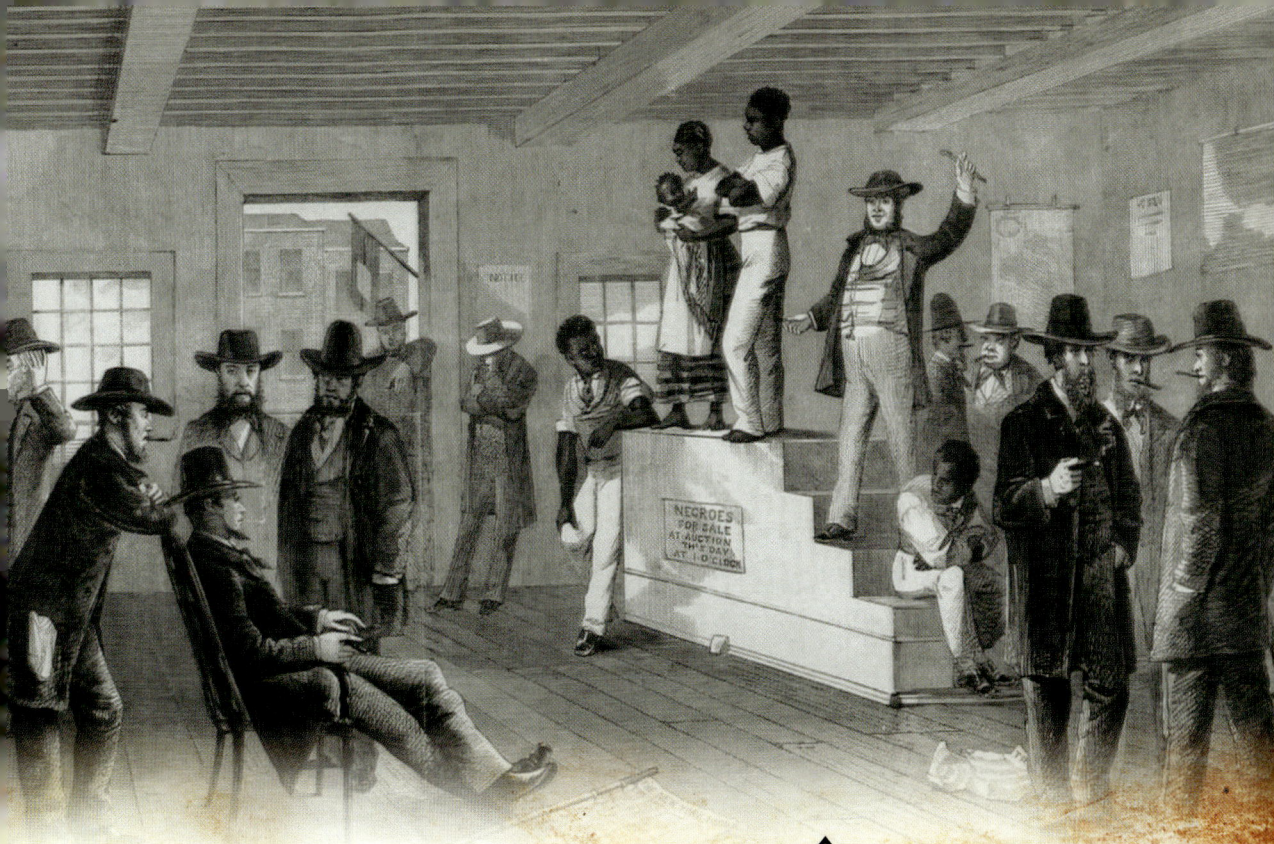

Slaves on sale in the Virginia state capital, Richmond.

A Kindly Owner

Because Nat was obviously intelligent, Benjamin Turner let him play with white children on the plantation. Nat learned to read and write, and studied the Bible. But Nat's childhood suddenly changed. His father ran away to the North and disappeared. Meanwhile, Benjamin Turner sold 360 acres (145 ha) of his land to his own son, Samuel. Samuel also took eight slaves, including Nat. In October 1810, when Nat was 10, Benjamin Turner died. Nat became Samuel's property.

In his little free time, Nat began to study religion. Slave religion in the South was a blend of traditional African beliefs and Christianity. Nat also began to have **visions**. He believed the visions were a sign from God that he must study the Bible harder in order to fulfill his **divine** purpose.

Gabriel's Rebellion

The best-known slave uprising before Nat Turner's also took place in Virginia. The state was home to some of the strongest supporters of slavery. In 1800, a freed slave and blacksmith named Gabriel Prosser planned a rebellion with his brother Martin, a slave preacher. The Prossers planned to rise up against whites in Richmond, Virginia. The brothers were influenced by the French and American revolutions. They agreed with the ideas that all men were born equal and had basic rights such as life, liberty, and the pursuit of happiness. Gabriel's rebellion failed when he was betrayed by black informers. The Prossers and their accomplices were arrested and later hanged.

The Prosser brothers were inspired by the ideas of the French Revolution, which began in 1789.

Hard Times

In 1819, the American economy suffered a financial crash caused by the effects of wars in Europe. The crash was felt particularly badly in the South. In Southampton County, some plantation owners chose to sell slaves they could no longer afford to keep. Samuel Turner, however, instead decided to work his slaves harder and harder.

In 1821, having been beaten, Nat ran away. After 30 days on the run, he came back to the plantation. He claimed to have had a vision in which he was told to return. The story made the other slaves suspicious of Nat. They began to think that he was a troublemaker.

A New Owner

Samuel Turner died in 1822, and his widow sold Nat and the other slaves. Nat's new owner, Thomas Moore, worked him even harder than Samuel Turner had done.

In the early 1800s, Virginia had only a few towns scattered among the plantations.

Nat had to do many jobs on the plantation, not just pick cotton. He became depressed. By 1825, he was convinced that he had to gain his freedom. He based this conclusion on his study of the Bible. He carefully read the Bible passages that slave owners said supported the idea of slavery. Nat decided that, in fact, the Bible taught exactly the opposite lesson.

As Nat's religious knowledge grew, he began preaching to Moore's other slaves. He preached about his visions. He told his congregation that Judgment Day was close at hand. His **sermons** became popular across the county.

A planter sells his possessions and slaves at an auction after the economic crash of 1819.

A Religious Man

Unlike his father, Samuel Turner did not single Nat out for special treatment. When Nat turned 12, Turner sent him to work in the fields with the other slaves. Nat was forced to do hard manual work, and was no longer allowed to play with white children. Turner did, however, allow Nat and the other slaves to attend a church he built for them, known as Turner's Meeting House. The preacher chose lessons from the Bible that stressed the importance of being an obedient slave. Instead, the young Nat began to believe that the Bible was giving him a different message: that he had a divine purpose to end slavery.

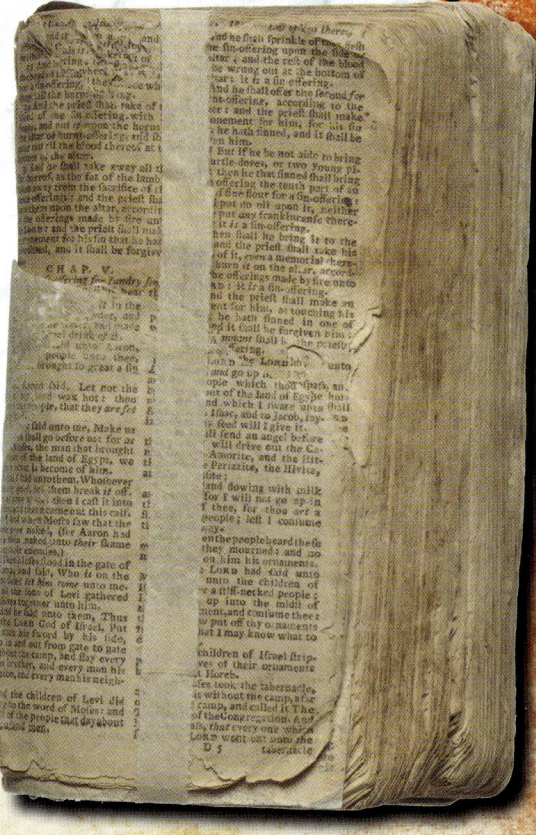

This is the Bible Nat Turner used for his preaching.

In 1827, Nat **baptized** a white man he had befriended. This was Etheldred Brantley. Brantley was a former slave owner who had lost everything through drinking too much. Brantley's white neighbors would not have anything to do with him, so Brantley mixed with Nat and the other slaves.

When news of the baptism spread, Nat became even better known for his religious activity. His fellow slaves took to calling him "The Prophet."

A Vision

On May 12, 1828, Nat had a new vision. It told him that he needed to fight against those who had **oppressed** him and made him a slave. The vision told him to remain quiet until God sent him a sign that he should start preparing for an uprising. Nat did not stay silent, however. He told his fellow slaves on Moore's plantation to get ready for freedom. When Moore heard what Nat had been saying, he beat him.

Shortly afterward, Moore died. His widow married a man named Joseph Travis, who took over the plantation. Nat became Travis's property. He continued to work hard as he waited for a sign from God that it was time to act.

Slaves prayed in the outdoors with slave preachers like Nat.

A Solar Eclipse

The solar eclipse Nat interpreted as a sign from God occurred on February 11, 1831. A solar eclipse happens when the moon passes between the sun and Earth, blocking the sun's light. As the moon passes in front of the sun, the light on Earth becomes dim.

The rays of the sun cause a halo behind the black disk of the moon.

The Sign Comes

Travis turned out to be a kind master who let Nat preach to the other slaves while they worked in the fields. After 2 years, however, everything changed.

On February 11, 1831, Nat believed he had received the sign he was waiting for. A **solar eclipse** took place above Virginia. In Nat's eyes, the shadow of the moon was like a black hand passing over the sun. Nat took this as a message from God. It was time to act.

DID YOU KNOW?
SOLAR ECLIPSES MAKE THE DAYLIGHT DIM ON EARTH. IN THE PAST, ANCIENT PEOPLES OFTEN BELIEVED ECLIPSES WERE SIGNS FROM THE GODS.

REBELLION!

In February 1831, Nat told four of his closest friends to prepare for a rebellion. The date he chose was July 4, Independence Day.

Nat asked his friends—his fellow slaves Hark, Henry, Nelson, and Sam—to begin to raise support for a rebellion. He wanted them to stir up **discontent** among other slaves in Southampton County. The more slaves who joined the uprising, he argued, the better the chances of success.

When July 4 arrived, however, there was no rebellion. Nat had made himself sick by worrying about his plans. He delayed the uprising until his health improved.

To be certain that he was doing the right thing, Nat waited for a second sign from God. It came on August 13, 1831. Again, the sun seemed to dim and it turned a blue–green color. Nat took this as a new sign that it was time to rise up against the slave owners.

Nat read it as a sign when the sun turned a blue-green color.

The rebels caught and ate a hog before they began their uprising.

The Rebellion Begins

On the night of Sunday, August 21, 1831, Nat and his followers met in some woods near the plantation. They deliberately chose a Sunday. Neither white people nor slaves worked on Sunday. It was common for slaves to spend the day hunting for extra food, so no one would think it was strange to see a band of male slaves away from their plantation.

With the addition of two slaves named Will and Jack, there were now seven rebels in all. After roasting and eating a hog, they were ready.

Nat's plan was simply to kill any white slave owners they could find. He made his followers agree that they would not spare anyone because of their age or sex. Beyond this plan, however, he had not really thought about what he would do if the rebellion succeeded.

A Volcanic Explosion

Historians now think the dimming sun that Nat Turner had interpreted as a second divine sign was caused by a volcanic eruption. Mount St. Helens, which is in what is now Washington State, was continually active during the mid-1800s. Experts today think that a plume of smoke and ash rising from the volcano probably darkened the sky across North America. It may have been smoke in the air that made the sun appear to change color.

Mount St. Helens is still active today. It last erupted in 1980.

The rebels used axes because guns were too noisy.

The First Victims

After midnight, the men made their way to the house of Nat's owner, Joseph Travis. The men were armed with axes and hatchets. They entered the house quietly so as not to wake the sleeping family.

As the **ringleader**, Nat had been chosen to strike the first blow. He brought his hatchet down on the sleeping Joseph Travis. The blow woke Travis before Hark killed him with more blows. The slaves then killed the other members of the family. The men stole some guns and then fled.

The Uprising Continues

Nat and the other slaves made their way to the next farm, which belonged to a man named Sal Francis. They killed everyone there and moved on to the home of a widow named Piety Reece.

DID YOU KNOW?
SLAVES OFTEN USED TOOLS SUCH AS AXES AND KNIVES FOR THEIR WORK, SO NO ONE WOULD THINK IT UNUSUAL FOR THE REBELS TO HAVE THEM.

The slaves killed Piety Reece and her son before moving on to the farm of Samuel Turner's widow, Elizabeth. As well as guns, they had also seized nine horses. They had not used their guns because they feared the sound would alert whites in the area. Instead, they killed their victims with axes.

The Group Splits

More slaves had joined the group during the night, so there were now 15 rebels in all. Turner split them into two groups. Things began to go wrong, however. One group of rebels arrived at the plantation of Richard Porter to find that the white owners had fled. Their slaves had warned them about the **insurrection**. The word was out.

The slaves killed everyone in the Sal Francis house.

This is a very dramatic image of an imaginary slave uprising.

Drunk!

Over the next 12 hours, the rebels continued to attack white farmers. They had killed around 60 white people on 15 farms, freeing any slaves as they went. Nat's band now numbered some 60 or 70 slaves. The rebels were not united, however. Some had stolen liquor from the houses they attacked. They soon became drunk. Other rebels became tired or scared, so they quit and went home.

By noon on August 22, the slaves had gotten as far as the nearest highway. Nat now intended to march to the county seat, Jerusalem, where there was an **armory**. He hoped to steal more weapons to arm his followers.

Slave Support

Nat Turner hoped more slaves would join his revolt, but many refused. The rebels found some farms and plantations deserted when they arrived because slaves had alerted their masters about the uprising. Some slaves may have done this from a sense of personal loyalty to their owners. Many others believed their masters when they told them slavery was the best thing for slaves.

↑ This glamorized image shows slaves and whites living happily together.

But Nat was finding it more and more difficult to control his bunch of rebels. Those who were drunk wanted to carry on drinking, while some of the others were fighting among themselves.

Race Against Time

Nat knew that word of the rebellion would be spreading. By now the auhorities would be calling out the **militia**. That evening, he and his men hid in the forest. They spent a restless night worrying that the militia would find them.

DID YOU KNOW?
THE MILITIA HAD ORIGINALLY BEEN ORGANIZED SO THAT REMOTE COMMUNITIES IN THE COUNTRYSIDE WERE PROTECTED FROM ATTACK.

Nat sent out a patrol to check for soldiers. When the patrol returned, many of the rebels mistook them for the militia and ran away. After these desertions, Nat was left with just 20 men. He knew that time was running out.

The Rebecca Vaughan House was the last place where anyone was killed by Nat and his rebel slaves.

FIGHTING AUTHORITY

The uprising caught the white population by surprise. Wild rumors spread about the size of the rebellion, and fear gripped Southampton County.

Nat Turner and the other rebels had started their rebellion with the advantage of surprise. By the morning of Tuesday, August 23, however, that advantage had been lost. After spending the night in the woods, Nat and his band set out for Jerusalem, the county seat. He hoped to find weapons and money there. He also hoped to **recruit** more slaves to his cause.

Nat and his followers discuss their plans in the woods.

↑ Slaves rebel against slave traders in Africa. Stories of slave violence terrified many whites in the South.

Making Mistakes

The rebels badly needed more **reinforcements**. Before heading to Jerusalem, they decided first to visit the plantation of Simon Blunt. They hoped to persuade some of Blunt's 60 slaves to join them. As they got close to the house, however, Blunt and another man opened fire with guns. One of the rebels was killed.

To make matters worse, Blunt's slaves had already decided that the uprising was doomed to failure. They chose to take the side of their master. Blunt's slaves attacked Nat's men with hoes and pitchforks and took some of them captive. As Nat fled from Blunt's plantation, his band of rebels was even smaller than it had been that morning.

Panic in Southampton County

By this time, slaves throughout the county were passing on news about Nat's insurrection. Panic spread among the white community. Rumors said that there were as many as 1,200 rebel slaves on the rampage.

Events were so confused that a story even began that the British had returned to invade the United States, as they had in the War of 1812 (1812–1815). Church bells rang across the county to warn residents about the uprising. The county authorities sent a request to the state capital, Richmond, asking for military help.

The first newspaper reports of the rebellion included illustrations showing what people thought had happened.

The State Militia

In the 1800s, many states maintained their own militia, especially in slaveholding states. These volunteers acted as a local military force to keep public order and to chase and capture escaped slaves. The Virginia militia was formed as early as 1607, when the American colonies were still under British control. It had ended up fighting against the British in the War of 1812.

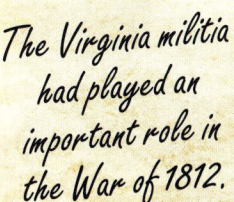

The Virginia militia had played an important role in the War of 1812.

The Militia Arrive

After being driven away from Simon Blunt's plantation, Nat and his remaining men fled back to the woods. They soon ran into units of local militia who were hunting for them. The militia opened fire on the slaves. Three rebels were killed, including Nat's friend Will. Nat now had only four companions left. The slave uprising he had dreamed about had been reduced to just five survivors.

A Final Stand

Nat sent two of the men, Curtis and Stephen, to try to recruit more slaves. Instead, they were stopped, arrested, and sent to jail. Meanwhile, Nat and his last two companions headed back to the Travis farm.

↑ This illustration shows Nat dreaming of an uprising against the whites.

Nat was still convinced that more slaves would join him. He believed that other rebels were hiding in the countryside, waiting for orders. Nat sent his last two companions to find them. Now he was alone. He took food from the abandoned Travis home and headed into the woods. His rebellion had lasted only 2 days.

The County Responds

While Nat was in hiding, the authorities organized their response. Reinforcements poured into Southampton County, as 800 **federal** troops joined 2,000 local militia. The militia were now organized, armed, and ready to fight the rumored slave army. Meanwhile, terrified white residents took the law into their own hands. They started to attack and kill free blacks and slaves as revenge for the uprising.

In one of the worst **atrocities**, white civilians rode through the countryside, killing around 40 black men and women over the course of 2 days. One group of riders killed 15 slaves and beheaded them. They stuck the heads on poles to act as a warning of what would happen to any other slave who might rebel.

Trials

With Nat Turner still at large, the authorities began trying the 49 slaves who had been captured. The trials started on August 31, 1831. The authorities were determined that the slaves would be found guilty, even if the evidence against them was weak. They wanted to make an example of the rebels to **discourage** any future uprisings.

Rewards were offered for the capture of rebellious slaves, as in this proclamation in 1839.

The court found three teenage slaves guilty of joining the rebellion even though they had been forced to join the other slaves and then held at gunpoint to stop them from running away. Three of Nat's gang—Sam, Hark, and Nelson—gave evidence of how they planned the rebellion with Nat. All the captured slaves were found guilty. They were sentenced to be hanged on September 9, 1831.

Where's Nat?

There remained the problem of the ringleader. Nat Turner was still on the run. Some people believed he must have left the state and escaped to the North or even to the Caribbean. Others thought that he must still be hiding in Virginia.

The governor of Virginia, John Floyd, offered a reward for anybody who could capture the missing slave. He offered $500 to anyone who brought Nat to the Southampton County Jail. The reward encouraged slave hunters to spend September looking for Nat, but they had no success. More people became convinced that Nat had fled the state. It would turn out that he had never left the county.

← Virginia governor John Floyd was eager to bring Nat Turner to trial.

The Proclamation

John Floyd's offer of a $500 reward for Nat's capture gave this description of the runaway slave:

"5 feet 6 or 8 inches high, weighs between 150 and 160 lbs. Rather 'bright' complexion, but not a mulatto [half-black, half-white], broad shouldered, large flat nose, large eyes, broad flat feet, rather knockneed, walks brisk and active, hair on the top of the head very thin, no beard except on the upper lip, and the tip of the chin, a scar on one of his temples, also one on the back of his neck, a large knot on one of the bones of his right arm, near the wrist, produced by a blow."

The governor's proclamation attracted many slave hunters to Southampton County.

DID YOU KNOW?

Slave hunters in the north tracked runaway slaves from the south in order to claim rewards for their capture and return.

DEFEAT AND LEGACY

Despite the huge manhunt in Southampton County, there was no sign of Nat. When he was found, it was not by a soldier or a slave hunter—but by a dog.

Nat Turner had been missing for 6 weeks. All that time, he had been hiding in a hole he had dug in a field. He had disguised the hole by covering it with some fence poles. Nat lived off the supplies he had taken from the Travis house. He was very careful not to risk being seen during the day. He only left his hole in the middle of the night to get water from a nearby creek.

Rotten Meat, Rotten Luck

The meat Nat had taken from the Travis house and was storing in the hole was

This is the first hole where Nat hid while on the run.

When Nat tried to surrender at Nathaniel Francis's house, Francis shot at him.

beginning to grow rotten. One day, a dog sniffed it and began to dig at the hole. Two nights later, while Nat was outside the hole, the same dog appeared and began to bark at him. The barking attracted the two slaves who were with the dog. Nat pleaded with the slaves not to give him away, but they later told their master what had happened. The search was back on.

On the Run

Nat went on the run to avoid the armed patrols sent out to find him. He realized that his luck had run out, and decided to give himself up to a white man named Nathaniel Francis. Nat had known Francis since he was a boy. Instead, Francis fired a gun at Nat, who ran off back into the woods. Once again, Nat was able to keep out of sight of the patrols, this time by hiding in a new hole beneath a fallen tree.

On October 30, 1831, a patrol passed through the woods without spotting him. When the patrol had gone, Nat climbed out of his hiding place to check on the sticks and leaves he was using to **camouflage** the hole.

Found!

Nat found himself face-to-face with a poor white farmer named Benjamin Phipps, who happened to be walking through the woods. Nat had a sword and Phipps had a gun. Nat agreed to drop his weapon if Phipps did not shoot him. Nat Turner's slave rebellion was over.

Nat comes face-to-face with Benjamin Phipps in the woods.

This house belonged to the county clerk at Nat's trial.

Taken to Jerusalem

Phipps set out to take Nat to the jailhouse in Jerusalem. As news of Nat's capture spread, the two men were soon surrounded by angry whites who threatened to kill Nat. Phipps put Nat in a local farmhouse overnight for his own protection. He finally took him to Jerusalem the next day.

Nat's trial was set for November 5, 1831. The court assigned him a defense attorney named Thomas Gray. As Nat waited for his trial, Gray visited him regularly in his jail cell. During their conversations, Gray persuaded Nat to give his own account of the rebellion. Gray later turned Nat's story into a famous book entitled *The Confessions of Nat Turner*.

The Trial

When the trial began, it did not last long. Witnesses described what had happened during the rebellion, but Nat had already confessed to plotting and carrying out the uprising. The verdict was inevitable. Nat Turner was found guilty of all the charges and sentenced to be hanged on November 11, 1831. As with the other slaves who had been executed after the uprising, the state valued Nat at $375. This was the amount the state would pay as **compensation** to his owner for the loss of property.

On November 11, Nat was hanged. When he was asked if he had any last words, he replied simply, "I'm ready."

Nat tells his story to Thomas Gray in his cell.

The Confessions of Nat Turner

After Nat's arrest, his attorney Thomas Gray used Turner's words to write *The Confessions of Nat Turner, the Leader of the Late Insurrections in Southampton*. Both men believed that publishing Nat's account would help his ideas survive for future generations. Nat hoped it would help people understand why he had begun the first slave rebellion in which white people had died.

Nat's story was published in 1832 and became a best seller.

DID YOU KNOW?
After Nat Turner's uprising, the fight to abolish slavery was largely carried on through peaceful attempts to change the law.

Nat's Skull

After his death, Nat's skull became separated from his skeleton. One story claims that the skull ended up at Wooster College, Ohio, in 1866. People were interested in criminals' skulls because of a theory that the size and shape of a skull influenced a person's character. In 1901, a fire destroyed the building holding the skull, but it was said to have survived. One hundred years later, it turned up in Gary, Indiana. In 2016 it was returned to Nat Turner's living descendants.

This is believed to be the skull of Nat Turner.

Legacy

Nat Turner's rebellion was a failure that only lasted 2 days. It had a lasting legacy, however. After Nat's death, the Virginia **legislature** thought about ending slavery in the state.

In the end, the legislature decided to do the opposite. It not only introduced laws intended to preserve slavery. It also introduced even more restrictions on slaves' lives. These laws tried to prevent future uprisings by forbidding slaves and free blacks from gathering together. This was intended to stop them from being able to plan rebellions. It also meant that it was now illegal for African Americans to go to church together. It was also made illegal for white people to teach any black people to read or write. In addition, blacks could no longer bear arms.

Toward War

These harsh measures widened the gulf between the growing antislavery feeling in the Northern states and the proslavery feeling in the South. The division would grow more bitter over the coming decades. In 1861, it would be a major cause of the conflict that threatened to destroy the United States, the Civil War (1861–1865).

A black unit in the Union Army during the Civil War.

TIMELINE

1794 The invention of the cotton gin by Eli Whitney means that more cotton can be grown and processed, increasing the need for slaves.

1799 Nat Turner's mother is bought by Benjamin Turner of Southampton County, Virginia.

1800 **October 2:** Nat Turner is born into slavery. Gabriel Prosser plans a slave rebellion in Virginia, but it is discovered before it begins.

1808 The US Congress bans the international slave trade.

1810 After Benjamin Turner dies, Nat becomes the property of Samuel Turner.

1819 A financial crash damages the Southern economy.

1821 Nat Turner runs away briefly. When he returns, he claims to have had visions from God.

1822 After Samuel Turner dies, Nat is sold to Thomas Moore.

1825 Nat begins preaching to his fellow slaves. He is convinced that he should try to gain his freedom.

1827 Nat baptizes a white plantation owner named Etheldred Brantley.

1828 **May 12:** Nat has a vision telling him that he must fight white slave owners.

1831

February 11: A solar eclipse takes place. Nat believes it is a sign from God to prepare for an uprising.

July 4: The rebellion planned by Nat and his friends is postponed because Nat is sick.

August 21: On a Sunday evening, Nat and his friends gather in the woods and eat before they begin their uprising.

August 22: Soon after midnight, the rebels begin attacking homes and killing white people. By the afternoon, the group has grown to 60 or 70 slaves, but many soon leave.

August 23: After trying unsuccessfully to recruit more followers, Nat goes into hiding. His fellow rebels are arrested.

August 31: The trials of the captured slaves begin.

September 9: The rebels are hanged.

September 17: Virginia governor John Floyd offers a reward of $500 for Nat's capture.

October 30: Nat Turner is discovered and captured by Benjamin Phipps.

October 31: Phipps delivers Nat Turner to the jailhouse in Jerusalem.

November 5: Nat Turner stands trial and is found guilty.

November 11: Nat Turner is hanged in Jerusalem.

1832 *The Confessions of Nat Turner* is published in Richmond, Virginia.

GLOSSARY

abolitionists: People who called for the end of slavery.

armory: A place where weapons and ammunition are stored.

atrocities: Extremely cruel and violent acts.

baptized: Made a member of the church by a ceremony of baptism.

camouflage: To make something blend in with its surroundings.

compensation: Money given to someone to make up for a loss.

cotton gin: A machine that mechanically separates the threads of the cotton plant.

discontent: A feeling of being dissatisfied with life.

discourage: To try to prevent someone from doing something.

divine: Describes something that is associated with a god.

economy: All of the financial activity, industry, and trade of a region or country.

federal: Related to the US government.

imported: Describes goods brought into a country to be sold.

insurrection: A violent uprising against authority.

legislature: The branch of a government responsible for making new laws.

militia: A military force of trained citizens.

necessary evil: A thing that is known to be bad but that is important.

oppressed: Unjustly kept in a state of hardship.

plantations: Large estates for growing crops.

racist: Based on the belief that one race is superior to another.

recruit: To get someone to join a cause or organization.

reinforcements: Additional people to strengthen a force.

ringleader: The person who begins or leads an action that breaks the rules.

sermons: Talks on religious subjects.

slavery: The state of being owned and forced to work.

solar eclipse: An astronomical event when the moon passes between Earth and the sun.

visions: Trances or dreams in which people see things.

FURTHER INFORMATION

Books

Burgan, Michael, and Richard Dominquez. **Nat Turner's Slave Rebellion. Graphic History.** Mankato, Minn: Graphic Library, 2006.

Gregson, Susan R. **Nat Turner: Rebellious Slave. The New Nation Biographies.** Mankato, Minn: Bridgestone Books, 2003.

Schmid, Katie Kelley. **Nat Turner and Slave Life on a Southern Plantation. Jr. Graphic African American History,** New York, NY: PowerKids Press, 2013.

Websites

http://www.facts-about.org.uk/famous-people-facts-starting-with-n/nat-turner.htm
A list of 15 facts for kids about Nat Turner.

http://news.nationalgeographic.com/2016/10/nat-turner-slave-rebellion-legacy/
An article from National Geographic with links to images of artifacts linked to Nat Turner.

http://www.american-historama.org/1829-1841-jacksonian-era/nat-turner-rebellion.htm
This page looks at the influence of Nat Turner's rebellion on the United States at the time.

http://www.learnnc.org/lp/editions/nchist-newnation/4574
The story of Nat Turner's rebellion from the North Carolina digital learning website.

Publisher's note to educators and parents: Our editors have carefully reviewed these websites to ensure that they are suitable for students. Many websites change frequently, however, and we cannot guarantee that a site's future contents will continue to meet our high standards of quality and educational value. Be advised that students should be closely supervised whenever they access the Internet.

INDEX

abolitionism 10

Bible, the 13, 16
Blunt, Simon 29, 31
Brantley, Etheldred 17

Civil War 43
Confessions of Nat Turner, The 39, 40, 41
cotton 5, 11
cotton gin 10, 11

eclipse, solar 19
economy, Southern 7, 9
economy, US 15

Floyd, John 34, 35
Francis, Nathaniel 37
Francis, Sal 23, 24
French Revolution 14

Gabriel's Rebellion 14
Gray, Thomas 39, 40, 41

Jamestown 4
Jerusalem, Virginia 25, 28, 39

militia 26, 27, 31, 32, 33
Moore, Thomas 15, 18
Mount St. Helens 22

Phipps, Benjamin 38, 39
plantations 5, 6, 7, 8
Porter, Richard 24

preaching, Nat Turner 16, 17, 19
Prosser, Gabriel 14

Rebecca Vaughan House 27
Reece, Piety 23, 24
religion 6, 13, 16, 17
Richmond 14, 30

Santeria 6
slave trade 5, 8, 9
slavery 4, 7, 11
slavery, legislation 42, 43
South, US 4, 5, 6, 7, 8, 9, 15
South Carolina 9
Southampton County 12, 15, 20, 32
sun, signs 19, 20

Travis, Joseph 18, 19, 23, 32
trials, of rebels 33, 34
Turner, Benjamin 8, 12, 13
Turner, Elizabeth 24
Turner, Nat
  capture 38, 39
  description 35
  skull 42
  trial 40
Turner, Samuel 13, 15, 17

uprisings, slave 14

Virginia 4, 13, 15, 42
visions, religious 15, 16, 17, 18, 32

War of 1812 30, 31